Everywhere Is North

poems by

Anne Hampford

Finishing Line Press
Georgetown, Kentucky

Everywhere Is North

for my mother

Copyright © 2021 by Anne Hampford
ISBN 978-1-64662-663-2 First Edition
All rights reserved under International and Pan-American Copyright Conventions. No part of this book may be reproduced in any manner whatsoever without written permission from the publisher, except in the case of brief quotations embodied in critical articles and reviews.

ACKNOWLEDGMENTS

I gratefully acknowledge the editors of the following publications in which these poems appeared, some in slightly different variations:

Constellations, A Journal of Poetry and Fiction: "Drake Passage"
Crab Creek Review: "Iceberg Garden"
Connecticut River Review: "Catastrophic Molt" and "Unresolved Stars"
Dogwood: A Journal of Poetry and Prose: "Short Talks: Antarctica"
Gulf Stream Magazine: "The Bridge"
Naugatuck River Review: "Antarctic Convergence" and "Wandering Albatross"
Not Very Quiet: "Crossings" and "True South"
River Heron Review: "Deception Island" and "From the Upper Deck"
Wild Roof Journal: "Circumpolar River"

NOTES

"Short Talks: Antarctica" is after Anne Carson's "Short Talks" from her collection *Plainwater, Essays and Poetry*

Publisher: Leah Huete de Maines
Editor: Christen Kincaid
Cover Art: Grace Donahue
Author Photo: Frédérique Tiéfry
Cover Design: Elizabeth Maines McCleavy

Order online: www.finishinglinepress.com
also available on amazon.com

Author inquiries and mail orders:
Finishing Line Press
PO Box 1626
Georgetown, Kentucky 40324
USA

Table of Contents

Wandering Albatross 1

Drake Passage 2

Catastrophic Molt 3

Krill 4

Circumpolar River 5

Ice Glossary 1 6

Iceberg Garden 7

Antarctic Convergence 8

Deception Island 9

Fresh Kill 10

Morning, Lemaire Channel 11

French Passage 12

Short Talks: Antarctica 13

Ice Glossary 2 14

Errera Channel 15

The Bridge 16

True South 19

Southern Right Whale 20

Portal Point 21

From the Upper Deck 22

Ice Glossary 3 23

Crossings 24

Form 25

To the Southern Ocean 26

Unresolved Stars 27

Southern Ocean Psalm 29

Return 30

First you fall in love with Antarctica, and then it breaks your heart.
   —*Kim Stanley Robinson*

Wandering Albatross

She swoops low over open ocean
swells, harnesses gravity for the windward
climb, leeward descent, turns

just above the water to rise again,
black-tipped wings rigid, white
feathers bright against the sea until

gone. They say an albatross can glide
for years without touching land, sleep
aloft. The wind as much a part of her

as tendon, bone. She'll return to where
she was born, stumble on spatulate feet
with her life mate, then leave to fly

alone. I can't survive on flight
but don't know where I'll land
next. Homesick for the unfamiliar.

Clumsy with what I know, eager
to defy gravity. Certain
only of my thirst for salt.

Drake Passage

I wake to twenty-foot swells, the ship
rolling in figure eights, slow
scrape of hangers,
drawers, me grasping. Lungs
burning. Outside, only
night and the heaving
sea. Land more
than a day away. This cabin
a coffin. How did I get here
where oceans meet and panic? I huddle
in the corner. Drown
in landlessness. Growing up,

dinner was at six sharp
every night, after
my father's two-olive
martini and the nightly
news. We sat in the same seats, ate
quickly. No seconds, no
leftovers. Table cleared, dishwasher
loaded, and dogs fed before
Jeopardy! at seven. My mother
knew the questions
to all the answers, asked me
nothing. I pinball aft

to open air, hold
tight to wet rails. Close
my eyes. Breathe
until the rhythm
of the waves is my own. Inhale,
exhale, dip, sway. My grip
loosens. The questions
keep coming.

Catastrophic Molt

How vocal and vulnerable they are, these penguins stained
in red krill, half-feathered and huddled on the melting

snow. They grow new plumage to survive the year. Three weeks
shore bound and awkward before returning to the sea. Thinner,

cleaner. Elegant. They ignore me hovering in the slush. Fully
clothed. Leaning into no one. Staining nothing. Beneath

the layers, my skin wrinkles, roughens. Dead cells slough
off, new cells look old. Stories preserved in scars, tags, sun

spots. I can't shed any of it. I forget I'm not young, tell myself
possibilities still exist. I learn another language. Nurse

a half-hearted longing to see more—the aurora borealis,
Petra, an Esmeraldas woodstar. I make lists. How many kinds

of alone are there? I want to be on fire, wet with the gak and squawk
of intimacy. Dirty dishes, morning breath, a floor that needs

sweeping. Me, aging. Naked. Tinting something. Seen.

Note: catastrophic molt is the process by which some water birds molt all of their feathers at one time

Krill

Everywhere is north.
Ice is life, is krill
in swarms visible
from space. Crackling fantasia,
cracking, feeding, dying, blob
of oneness packed tight.
How do they know
where to go? Do they recognize
the open mouth and swim in anyway?
I never see them whole. Only
their detritus. Spit up
and shit out. Red husks stain
a white world, flecked
with penguin.

What have I sacrificed? His blue eyes, his swirling
touch. Certainty. The only evidence of me—a lover's
memory. Bones in earth.

Circumpolar River

I understand what grows in the scrape
left by icebergs on the sea floor. You were not

a beginning or an ending but the thick
middle of circling and circling, trying to gauge

depths and edges, the topography of growing
up and goodbye. You might have been

a seed in this white desert, eager
to sprout. I was a vessel that couldn't

hold you. Watertight. No room for the tiny
bubble of ancient air making the ice

as blue as your father's eyes. An ecosystem
without regret, I orbit the cold emptiness

of what you might have been. Filled
with questions, coming to terms

with memory and consequence. Changed
by glacier, growler, circumpolar river.

Ice Glossary 1

        anchor ice

                floats and clings

buoyancy
    fights

        gravity

                    I travel
                a world

    bergy-bits
        scattered white

              stars

on the dark sea
        my mother's last

            breath

    brash ice

            wreckage spewed

  blocking bays
  and channels

  strange   solace

Iceberg Garden

They call it a garden but it's not orderly,
not precise like my mother's beds:
pink foxglove along the fence, dawn roses
latticed through the back gate, yellow
peonies where the willow used to be.
The icebergs are scattered, each its own
species in a field random and wild.
Rippled sheets of gumdrop green.
An aqua-striped pinnacle beyond the dry-dock
edged in cobalt blue. Variegated whites
strewn to the horizon. Nothing seems to move.
No petal flutter or leaf quiver.
But they drift in the moving sea.
An almost imperceptible shifting
of something, a fragment of a whole
I'll never see. She didn't leave much
to chance. Coffee with cream
and a crossword for breakfast,
the company of her dogs, dying
in her own bed, a vase of red tulips
on the nightstand.

Antarctic Convergence

The dolphins are gone but the landscape
looks the same. Blue-gray sky and sea. Petrels.
We've entered the Southern Ocean, left
behind the current that defines it.

When Dad was dying, no longer scaffolded
by the calendar, he sometimes thought
I was his mother, became a child again.
Talked of the big house on Mahantongo Street.
"Why did we move?" I make up something
about walking to Yuengling's for CMP sundaes.
He quiets.

This ocean has no fixed boundaries. Shape
and location are dependent on pack ice and the way
cold water merges with warmer.

He sometimes thought I was his wife, my mother,
who wasn't supposed to die first. He pats my forearm
remembers the T-bird with the top down, driving
along the Schuylkill River, promises made. He closes
his eyes, drifts, thinks we are on the QE2 at cocktail hour.
"Where's my martini? They always forget my martini."

The current is a seam, shifting.

Sometimes he knew he was dying
and recognized me—"Oh, Annie, my
Annie, you'll take care of everything, won't you?"

Three oceans meet and merge, become part
of the bankless river circling the continent.
A kelp gull appears to starboard, orange-beaked
and calling as dolphins bound in our wake.

Deception Island

Ash and snow zebra the hills above
the flooded caldera, refuge
from icebergs and storms. The shore
littered with rusted whaling machinery, the shells
of buildings, boats, and krill. Fur seals
sleep cozied up to the metal waste. Layers

of eruption, carnage, calm. We were best friends
in high school. Hung out in her dark
house, yellow lightbulbs in every room. The Dead
on the stereo while we tried to make sense
of Kafka, blackheads, heartbreak. She sewed
her own clothes, baked brownies and let me eat

the batter. She was homecoming queen, I was eager
to leave. We'd get stoned and roam the nearby
woods. Once, we spent hours in a meadow singing
jingles. Laughing and dancing with the thistle, summer
berries, all the birds we didn't know. An edge
of wildness, we lay exhausted, the tall grass

scratching. She shed me when she shed herself,
anorexic and adamant. I didn't understand
erasure, didn't recognize pain
in her brown eyes. What else
had I missed? I climb up to the rim
for a view of the sea, life on the exposed

side of the island. Hairgrass. Chinstraps. The air
heavy with guano and gakking. The wind
pushes me back.

Fresh Kill

In one explosive move, the leopard seal snatches the gentoo penguin from below, bites hard and sucks out the innards, splattering the sea red. Mammal tosses bird into air, is gone before the splash of carcass on water. Prey eviscerated. Beak and feet intact. Empty. Floating. Face up, eyes open. The gentoo looks alive before it sinks into obsidian. The loss of what it held making it heavier, not lighter. The weight of me now manageable.

Morning, Lemaire Channel

Sea spray scours, I lean into the vocal cold. Dawn
metallic. Kelp gulls. Prions. This ship journeys

south. Long ago, I promised you that we would come here
to see adelies and the albatross that stays aloft for years—

but I loved someone else instead. The wind
gusts; I brace myself against the deck rail, eyes

on the ice-blinked horizon, waiting
for nothing. The air smells clean, bites a bit.

I've traveled farther without you. *Brash, floe,
growler, spicule.* So many forms, one molecule.

French Passage

65° South, the wind at forty knots. Icebergs
silhouetted in morning gray: the world
in negative. A petrel glides by, becomes
fog. The ship holds steady towards

French Passage and the continent. When
I went away to college, my father drove
me in the family station wagon. Five hours
with few words. No advice or chitchat. He

focused on the road. I counted the mile markers
to freedom. We pulled up to the dorm, unloaded
onto the sidewalk—one trunk, two suitcases,
my stereo and albums. He gave me a quick

hug, pressed a crisp $100 bill into my hand, hopped
in the car, and drove away. I stood there
in my buffalo sandals and braids watching
the space where the car had been, unable

to move. Unsure of what had just happened.
Now, I stand on the ship's upper deck—
brash ice and bergy-bits block the passage.
Beyond the entrance, a garden

of icebergs—pinnacles and flat tops in deep
blues and bright whites, but this is
as close as we'll get. The ship can go
no further. The helmsman calls

the headings: one four zero, we turn toward
the peninsula; one three zero, mountains appear, ringed
in clouds; one two zero… precise navigation
for the vessel's measured turning.

Short Talks: Antarctica
Variations on a Theme by Anne Carson

On Independence

Yellow-flowered, herbaceous, and cushiony, Antarctic pearlwort survives the extreme cold of 60°S with little sunlight, moisture, or good soil. Growing in the rocks and relying on the wind to bring pollen, often from one of its own flowers, it doesn't need much else.

On Determination

Lush, layered, and slow-growing, Antarctic mosses live on meltwater, then survive without it for months, desiccating almost completely and retaining heat even in the frigid winter. They can be revived with exposure to light after being frozen, and seemingly dead, for a thousand years.

On Relativity

Compressed ice, ancient air trapped within, scatters and transmits the short waves of white light and absorbs the long ones. The bluer the ice, the older its stories.

On Patience

Antarctic lichens are colorful, composite organisms, a symbiosis between a fungus and alga that can photosynthesize while frozen and are the first colonists on bare rock. They grow at a glacial pace—as little as one centimeter every thousand years in harsher environments.

On Survival

A fine-leafed, vascular plant, Antarctic hair grass is tufted and grows in rocky areas. It can withstand the disturbance of elephant seals, wind, and penguin guano without withering away. A deep and complex root system keeps it anchored and nourished.

Ice Glossary 2

floe

floating frozen

on what
 I
once was

home
has many forms

frazil
 Dad's dementia

fingers dangling

in the untamed

sea

growler

ice awash

peeks above

the churning surface
what

ghosts me

Errera Channel

I'm freezing my ass off on the upper deck, thinking about my mother folding laundry and Pachelbel's Canon in D Major, which reminds me of my father, who loved classical music, especially Tchaikovsky and a full orchestra (gotta have a brass section), but this channel is baroque—the sea, the sea reflecting clouds and mountains, icebergs, then the mountains and clouds, then, the dawn sky the color of the sea in layered hues that remind me of fire and smoke, if smoke was precise and fire was kind and both were perfectly tuned. The snowy peaks are bass notes, not dark but essential like water, which surrounds me now in its different forms: liquid, solid, memory. Which is to say, I forgive the cold.

The Bridge

shuga frazil nilas
brash—the helmsman recites
types of ice

what wind can do
to water—

    the sea has large wavelets

        crests begin to break

foam is glassy

      scattered white horses

•

fluent in something other
    than longing   whale song

or engine whine—sounds that don't crush
    my ribcage

        an iceberg calves   the crackle
    and echo come later

last night I dreamed   a non-linear language

    my hair combed wet
with snow and ash

      red-gold tresses like feather grass—

    a cupboard opening to a coastline
    elastic with ice—

cowrie shells whispering kelp secrets
                    at the base of a prayer tree—

    a relief map   with contour lines of lotus silk
    shaded in nutmeg and neroli—

terraced fields   a strawberry-lined aqueduct—

my mother's head cupped in my hand
    her handwriting an ocean

    a threshold—

a landscape of sapphire
    and turmeric on a paint-splattered wall

    a hanging nest   holding memory and dew—

      my true name etched on a door
    adorned with pearlwort and prime numbers

    it was knobless—

time   a stringless kite
    she's been dead for fifteen years—

it's tomorrow and yesterday
    and right now   all at once—

    waiting in the corner   the three imaginary friends
                      from my childhood

        how did they know

          •

these bones
daughtering

nails bitten
to the quick

no blood
only tulips

yet

•

my mother's last words
no more talking

this ship's calligraphy

silver shards on scattered white horses
ice-blink igniting the horizon

the helmsman's voice in my ear—

polynya

slush

hummock

crevasse

True South

No true north
for me. No point
of orientation, fixed
and prophetic. I'm drawn
to what throws me off
balance. From this headland
above Penola Strait, I count
tussocks, petrels, and penguins.
The wind blusters my jacket
as I inhale the salt and guano air.

All these names to claim
the barrenness: Crystal
Sound, Errera Channel,
Pendleton Sea, traveler,
woman. Even the air
disorients. Lichen
and moss speckle
the dark rocks white
and green. I won't learn
their names.

Their strange presence
a challenge. I am my own
compass. Imprecise. Iceburn,
the needle of longing.

Southern Right Whale

The fifty-ton acrobat erupts
from the sea, a mass of black and white,
blubber and callosities, breaching

again and again. Every leap
a joyous dispatch of barnacles and
here I am. Every splash, the leviathan's

decree: *fin yourself, feed, trust
with abandon!*

Portal Point

With a shudder and barely a splash, the bergy-bit breaks away, pauses as if deciding what to do, then flips, revealing its ancient underside, the color of a Morpho butterfly. It begins to drift.

He's the one I never think about. His eyes weren't blue but they were kind and gentler than I was used to. I told him I loved him. Precise and patient, he cooked bouillabaisse, gave me a red toolbox and September peaches. Sliced and latticed the flesh, scooped out the pulp with deft fingers. He knew all my soft places but showered immediately afterwards. He dreamed of a gabled porch with two rocking chairs and the whir of a ceiling fan. I wanted a clean goodbye. Then I was the one floating north, picking up speed on the outgoing current.

From the Upper Deck

She made albums of her travels with my father. Sorted
and organized matchbooks, menus, a small watercolor
of St. Stephen's Green still wrapped in yellowed

cellophane. Wrote detailed narratives
in her Catholic school cursive—red chiffon
waltzing on the QE2, black coffee

and solitude at a Florentine café,
the Winter Palace. She filled
the leather-bound books with a life beyond

the house on Maymont Lane. Finished
the last one from her bed and didn't get up
again. At the end, she was barely

a paperweight on the sheets as she watched
her thoughts dwindle, hated
that emptiness. Then she was gone.

I ignore the cold wet of the deck rail, my hands
numb in the Antarctic wind. Not even an iceberg
interrupts the gray expanse of water and sky.

With nothing to orient by, I become my own
reference point, heed the scratch and brine. Stare
at the blankness until it quilts into troughs and crests,

a surface current pulling east. Brown kelp
surges past, tentacled, amorphous.
A part of me barnacled, homeward.

Ice Glossary 3

                                        ice-blink
                                            light reflected

    silvering
clouds
        skin soft

                                        and veinless

                 spicules

skeletal
      crystalline

                 water
                     in water

                                    my tongued heritage

tabular berg

                                                    adrift

                clean lines
                    in chaos

       where gravity
          betrays

Crossings

Drake Passage, Antarctic Circle,
the threshold of old age. Sea ice
doubling the continent in winter.
Glaciers make me feel young.
Another journey, the same
restlessness. Ice melts. Water
gives way. I'm always almost there.
What is this fear? I stare it down.
Only flinch a little.

Form

I'm floating in the warm saltwater pool,
main deck, sternward, snow prickling my face,

ship swaying, engine vibrating. I hear the cold.
Feel buoyant. Part in, part out. A surface,

something beneath it. This body has stories:
calloused feet and muscled thighs, my right hip

aching from all those miles; scars
on my inner calf from the yak that gored me

and a lover's scratch. I've seen an avalanche,
survived a whiteout. Did I fear the cold then?

I have my mom's nose and laugh lines. Our brows
creased with different kinds of loneliness. Hers curled

on the sofa with a book and two dogs. Mine, in bed
with the unfamiliar. I cradled my dad before

he died, let him call me "mother." I'm wrinkled
in five languages. Fluent in only one. Floating. Beyond

the stories. Because of them. Unanchored
and rocking, rocking, rocking. I want

to be touched and left alone, to hover
at the edge and know the depths. Prepared

for goodbye. On the way to brine, ice,
another form.

To the Southern Ocean

you got me with—

those blues   cyan   azure   cobalt
       shades that just don't belong in the cold

your shapeshifting   liquid   solid   vapor
       like you wouldn't bore me

the way the light hit   waves   bergs   fog banks
       showing off your best angles

and your music   cry and splash,
                    calving crackle, moaning tides
                    even the gakking of your damned penguins

I was willing to ignore your temper—
       all that howling and rolling
            that left me bruised and puking

and your vanity—
       how many photos of you must a girl take

but when you gave me—
       the night sky, thick
            with moon and stars, mirrored
on your liquid skin until
       there was no firmament, no ocean,
only light and movement that seemed
            like stillness and I was part of it, I forgot
my bones, my face. I lost
       my name.

Did you think I could trust that?

Unresolved Stars
    South Shetland Islands

Milky Way, sacred river, bridge
    between heaven and earth, guide
        and protector—

you're smothering the sky
    with too many stars, like all that cream
        in my mother's coffee.

        Is she out there with you?

I can't find Orion.
    Maybe I'd sleep better
        if I could.

In my half-dreams, I create constellations—

        a white eagle rushing the ecliptic,
            Jupiter in its beak;
        an elephant, trunk
            raised, black hole eye
        aflame;
        Pegasus unwinged.

There's so much I'll never know
    and you're still birthing stars—

        *

Reveal the dark spaces—

    where home is not a memory; it's algal
        and alive like the lake of my youth—

    where my mother's last cup
        has yet to be dried and put away—

    where longing no longer dogs me.

Let me feel the dark and become it,

    thick with unseen movement,
        evidence of the light rather than the light itself.

Show me stillness, despite the wind.

    *

On the eastern horizon,
    a pinnacle iceberg in silhouette
        there's ancient air inside—

        What can hold eternity?

I begin to see the sea ahead
    the way it quilts and crests
        but keeps going—

Your fading with the hint of day,
    one more thing
        before you go—

Keep me in this quiet orbit
    unhurried by gravity
        or regret—

    ready for

        gull cry

            silence

                whales breaching at dawn—

Southern Ocean Psalm

humpback orca minke sei
algae moss tussock moraine

spindrift wavelets ripples crests
crabeater leopard weddell ross

adelie chinstrap gentoo king
albatross petrel prion tern

neko gerlache detaille charcot
glacier growler frazil floe

Return

The Drake is calm. It's like Lake Aspetuck in summer.

*

I'm sixteen and floating. Away from shore, the strange
constellation of family. Alone. A hint of baby oil
in the air. I hover half in, half out, barely
rippling the surface. I'm a tiny current pointed
everywhere. There are worlds drifting
just outside of my awareness, like the lawn mower

humming somewhere on shore. I want to know
who I am. I'm in no hurry. A sunfish nibbles
my toes but I don't flinch.

Let it taste me!

*

I'm bare-armed on the upper deck, glad to feel warm sun
on this sixty-year-old skin. Antarctica is behind me.

*

The summer before my mom died, I'd visit her
at the lake. We'd sit in her garden, watch
the birds. She let me massage her feet. My rough
hands looked old beside their violet smoothness. She
could only bear the lightest of strokes.

Once I took her out in the canoe. The life jacket
engulfed her as I paddled us to the shaded cove, past
Sherman's rope swing, to the far end where algae grew
unchecked and eels nested in the rocks. We drifted

in lazy circles toward the center. A panorama of firsts
and lasts. *I should have learned to swim*, she said, steel

in her voice. She never asked me to teach her. The wind
pushed us back home—I only needed to steer.

*

A kelp gull alights on the ship's prow, preens its wings, chest, and tail.
White feathers spiral in the wind.

*

One July afternoon when I was seven, I found
my neighbor's infant face down and unmoving
in the water. She felt boneless when I plucked her
out. At last she coughed and sputtered; her body
went rigid; she breathed.

Sometimes a dead bluegill would wash up
on shore, slick-scaled and staring. Or the scraggle
of bones and feathers that used to be a mallard.

*

The icebergs are gone: nothing interrupts the sea.
We're more than a day away from land,
a thousand meters to the bottom.

*

In winter, the pines around the frozen lake seemed taller
and more vigilant, their branches pointing. The ice

along the shoreline was knotted and nubbed, crackling
in the thin places. It claimed beach and rocks,

everything the water touched. Grew into a crust
around the smooth black ice so dark it should've been

liquid. A foot thick with visible secrets: a maple leaf,
reddish and perfect with its curved petiole; small pebbles

that didn't belong; a striped bass, one eye watching
through glass. Riding thunderclaps of expansion

and contraction, I'd skate from end to end. The surface
a giant membrane of sound. My body a chord

composed of chimney smoke and snowdrifts.
Pretending I wasn't afraid, I went faster.

*

A cormorant bobs on the sea. Dives. Resurfaces
far ahead. Seems to run
across the water as it tries
to get airborne,
wings flapping hard.

*

Aspetuck was drained to repair the dam the autumn before she died. I walked where the water had been, the earth was dried and cracked with deer tracks, pine needles. Near the dam, a foot of pungent silt. The deep middle was lined with jagged boulders, shot through with quartz. Underground springs pooled into mud puddles, thick with rotting leaves. Golf balls and flip-flops, ageless in the muck. Vultures. A possum carcass.

There were bones: the skull of a small mammal, fish vertebrae, the skeleton of a bird wing. The lake smaller without its water.

When she died in the spring, it was still empty.

*

limbs heavy in the afternoon sun

I fall asleep   dream of tending

    my mother's body—

    sponging her limbs and torso with warm water
         to purify for the heaven she was sure awaited her

    oiling her skin with myrrh
         my hands saying goodbye
         to face, fingers, feet
         in steady rhythmic strokes

    wrapping her tight in linen
         to keep her safe

    I place my palms on her closed eyes
         make her names my prayer

            Tee

                                      Clare

  cirque

                mother

       *

I wake to low sun and the wind
rising; a wandering albatross
glides overhead. We're returning
to where we began, Cape Horn
just ahead but not yet
in sight. Beyond, more
north: solid ground
and warmth. The passage
is calm and filled with
questions. Memory
will edit out the cold, forgive
the rest. I'm still.

Anne **Hampford** is based in Connecticut but spends most of the year on the coast of Ecuador. Her poems have appeared in *Connecticut River Review, Crab Creek Review, Dogwood: A Journal of Poetry and Prose, Gulf Stream Magazine, Naugatuck River Review,* and *Wild Roof Journal,* among others. She holds a B.A. in Political and Social Thought from the University of Virginia and an M.A. in Comparative Literature from Rutgers University. She has traveled to six continents and can fake her way through several languages. This is her first chapbook of poetry.

www.ingramcontent.com/pod-product-compliance
Lightning Source LLC
LaVergne TN
LVHW041553070426
835507LV00011B/1073